Movement

Hilary Devonshire

FRANKLIN WATTS

New York/London/Toronto/Sydney

© Franklin Watts 1992

Franklin Watts, Inc.
95 Madison Avenue
New York, N.Y. 10016

Library of Congress Cataloging-in-Publication Data

Devonshire, Hilary.
    Movement / by Hilary Devonshire.
    p.   cm. — (Science through art)
    Includes index.
    Summary: Explains the basic scientific principles of movement
through experiments using art. Projects include windmills, a jack-in
-the-box, and concertina books.
    ISBN 0-531-14229-9
    1. Motion—Juvenile literature.   2. Motion—Experiments—Juvenile
literature.   3. Force and energy—Juvenile literature.   4. Force and
energy—Experiments—Juvenile literature.   [1. Motion—Experiments.
2. Force and energy—Experiments.   3. Experiments.   4. Art and
science.]   I. Title.   II. Series: Devonshire, Hilary.   Science
through art.
QC133.5.D48   1993
531—dc20   92-7837
                                                                 CIP AC

Series Editor: Hazel Poole
Edited by: Cleeve Publishing Services Limited
Design: Edward Kinsey
Artwork: Aziz Khan
Photography: Chris Fairclough
Consultants: Henry Pluckrose, Margaret Whalley

Typeset by Lineage, Watford

Printed in the United Kingdom

CONTENTS

This book describes activities which use the following:

Adhesives – cold water paste (for example wallpaper paste)
– acrylic PVA
Adhesive tape
Ball (styrofoam)
Beads
Blocks (wooden)
Board (long, for a ramp)
Bottle tops (plastic)
Brushes – for glue and paints
Candle (small)
Cardboard
Compass
Craft knife
Crayons
Cutting board
Dishwashing liquid bottle
Drinking straws (plastic)
Elastic
Felt-tip pens
Fun Tak
Inks (printing)
Knitting needle (metal)
Leaves
Masking tape
Modeling clay
Nail
Needle (sewing)
Oak tag (white and colored)
Paints

Paper – colored adhesive-backed paper
– colored construction paper
– white
– ¼ and ½ inch graph paper
Paper clips
Paper fasteners
Pen (black, waterproof)
Pencil
Pins – drawing pins
– headed pins
Protractor
Rod – dowel (wood)
– balsa wood
Roller (printing)
Rubber bands
Ruler – wooden or plastic
– metal safety ruler (for use with the craft knife)
Sand
Scissors
Sticks (wooden meat skewers)
Stopwatch
String (thin)
Thread
Tray
Wire (thin, for example, florist's wire)
Yarn (or fur)
Yogurt cup

INTRODUCTION

If we look around at things in our world we notice that there are many that move. Some things move because they have an energy of their own. They are self-propelled. Animals can move in many different ways. Some move on land, some move in water, some move in the air. Think how many different ways people can move. We have many words to describe these actions – leaping, running, walking, climbing, and there are many more.

Other objects, however, need a force to act upon them to make them move. They may be pushed or pulled, blown or thrown, lifted or turned. They may have an engine that makes them move. Look carefully at something that is moving. It may be moving in more than one way at the same time. There could be several forces acting upon the object in different directions. For example, the engine of a car will drive the car forward in a straight line, but it can also be steered to the right or left by the driver. A seed may be pulled toward the ground by gravity, but it may also be blown in another direction by the wind. When you study a moving object, try to discover how it is being moved, and how it is moving.

By following the investigations in this book you will learn something about the science of movement. At the start of each section there are some scientific ideas to be explored. You will be a scientist. A scientist looks at ideas and tries to discover if they are always true, and will also investigate to see if they can be *disproved*. A scientist tests ideas, makes investigations and experiments, and tries to explain what has happened. Your results may be surprising or unexpected, and you may find that you will need to make a new investigation or test a new idea.

You will also be an artist and designer. In each section you will be designing models, and through working with the various materials and techniques, you will make discoveries about how things move. Your finished artwork, designs, and models will be a record of your scientific findings.

STRAIGHT-LINE MOVEMENT

A push or pull on an object can make it move. It can also make it stop moving. A large force is needed to move a heavy object. A light object can be moved easily.

If there is only one force acting upon the object, then the object will move in a straight line in the direction of the force.

Mark out a straight line on the ground. You can move along the line forward or backward. If the ground is level, you are moving horizontally. If you climb up or down a gymnastics rope, you are moving in a vertical line.

An elevator moves up and down. Heavy cables provide the force to move it in a vertical line.

A train can move only in the direction of the rails on which it runs.

A card-pull picture

You will need: oak tag, paper, a ruler, scissors, a pencil, crayons, a craft knife and metal safety ruler, paste, and a brush.

1. Cut a strip of oak tag 1 inch wide. Draw and color a ship and glue it to the center of your strip.

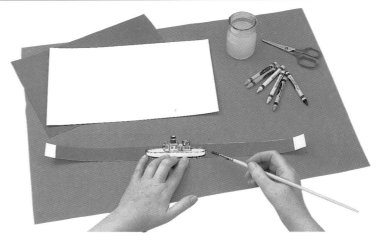

2. Cut two slits 1 inch long at both sides of a sheet of oak tag (size 11×14 inches) and thread the strip through the slits so that it slides sideways with ease.

3. Decorate your background with colored paper or crayons. You can make waves and clouds. Pull the strip at either side and watch your ship move. Notice how it moves only in a straight line. Try to think of an idea for an up-and-down moving picture.

A moving wagon

You will need: paper, oak tag, thin sticks, glue, a pencil, a craft knife, a metal ruler, four plastic bottle tops, a plastic drinking straw, a metal knitting needle, a small candle, thread and adhesive tape.

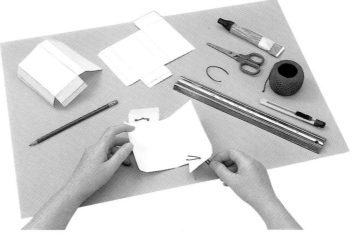

1. Draw a paper plan for the body of your wagon. Fold your pattern to see where you need to place tabs to join your model.

Transfer your design to oak tag. Score (do not cut) along the lines so that the oak tag folds easily. Make a hole in the center of each end of the wagon and push through a small loop of thread. Attach the loops into position with adhesive tape.

2. Glue the body together. Carefully warm the tip of the knitting needle in the candle. Melt a small hole in the center of the four bottle tops. These are the wheels. Rest the hot needle on a block of wood to cool.

WARNING: ASK AN ADULT TO LIGHT THE CANDLE. DO NOT TOUCH THE TIP OF THE NEEDLE. IT WILL BE VERY HOT.

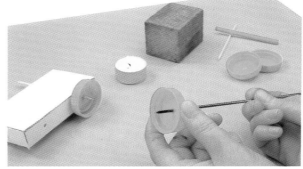

3. Use the thin sticks as axles. Place a small piece of drinking straw between each wheel and the body. Glue the wheels so that they are straight on the axles. Join a string pull to the front of the wagon.

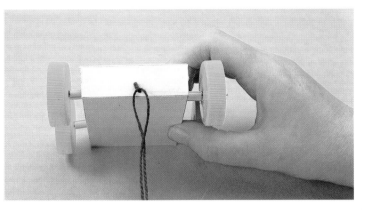

4. To test your wagon, place it at one end of a line and pull the string in the direction of the line. Because the wheels and axles are rigid and do not turn, the cart can only move straight forward.

Push the wagon in the other direction with a rigid stick. Remember, the push should be straight, and in the direction of the line.

5. Complete your model by making it into a vehicle of your own design. Color it with felt-tip pens.

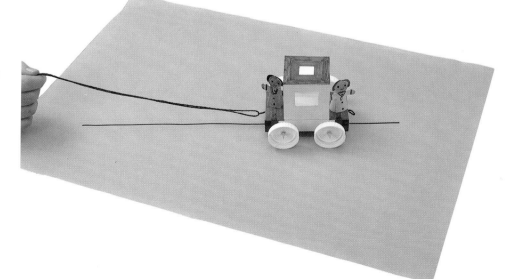

CIRCULAR MOVEMENT

If an object is fixed at one point it can turn around the point but cannot move away from the point. This turning movement, or rotation, is circular. When the object has rotated in one full circle it returns to the starting point. It may also rotate in the opposite direction.

An object can also move around a fixed point. If it stays at the same distance from the point it will move in a circle with the point at the center.

If you spin on the spot, you are rotating on a fixed point.

The hands of a clock move around a fixed point.

Stand on one spot with your arms outstretched. If you turn on the spot your hands will move in a circle. You can also make your hands move in a circle by standing still and just turning your arms from the shoulder.

See how many things you can think of that rotate in a circle. For example, the hands of a clock, or the wheels of a car.

Watch a potter working at the wheel. Notice how the potter centers the clay. As the wheel spins, the potter shapes the clay.

Drawing a circle

You will need: a drawing pin, string, and a pencil.

1. Work on a soft surface, such as a piece of cardboard on a thick pile of newspaper.

Make a loop with a piece of string. Affix the loop with the drawing pin and draw with the pencil, keeping the loop outstretched. The loop will hold the pencil at the same distance as it moves all the way around the pin.

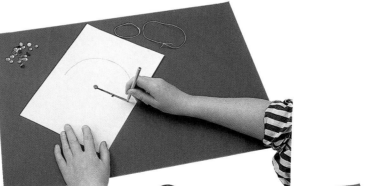

2. Experiment with a loop and two drawing pins. This time you will draw an ellipse, a rounded shape which is longer than it is wide. The earth moves around the sun on an elliptical orbit.

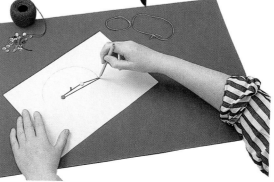

3. "Circle Fun"
Try colored pens or pencils
with loops of different sizes.
The drawing pins are at the
centers of the circles.

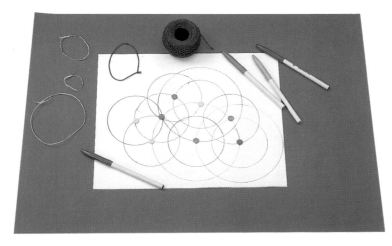

Circle patterns

You will need: paper, oak tag, a
paper fastener, and a pen or
pencil.

1. Cut out an irregular oak tag
shape. With a paper fastener,
attach one end of your shape to
the center of the sheet of paper.

2. Draw around the edge of
your shape. Move the shape a
short distance and draw around
the shape again. Do this until
you have a complete circular
pattern. Remove the fastener
and oak tag shape.

3. The finished design will
depend upon how far you move
your shape each time.

You can color your pattern
with felt-tip pens.

See what would happen if you
put the fastener in another
position on your oak tag shape.
You could try attaching the
fastener at the center of the oak
tag.

Experiment with this idea
using regular shapes – such as a
square, or a triangle.

A nosy elephant

This elephant was cut from oak tag. His trunk is attached to the head at one point with a paper fastener. Notice how it moves.

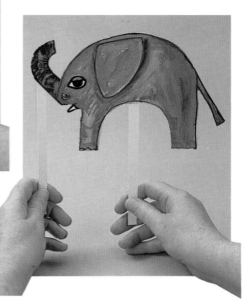

A hanging mobile

You will need: oak tag, a pencil, scissors, a craft knife and safety ruler, a dowel rod, and thread.

1. Use scissors and a craft knife to cut out some oak tag shapes. (Always hold the oak tag so that you cut *away* from your holding hand.)

2. Tie a thread to your shapes and to the center of the rod.

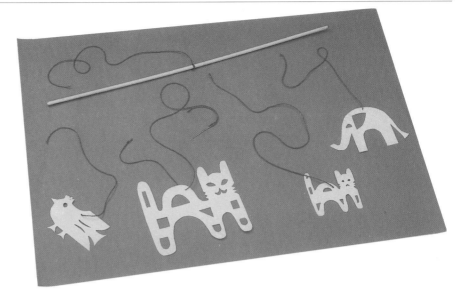

3. Hang your shapes on the rod so that they balance and the rod hangs horizontally. See how the mobile turns if you hang it in a drafty place.

SPIRALS

A spiral curves continuously around a fixed point (like the circle), but the distance from the point increases as the spiral grows.

A spiral can be drawn on a flat surface. If a flat spiral is cut along the length of the curve it will open into a three-dimensional curve. This curve is cone-shaped.

Some three-dimensional spirals are cylinder shaped, like a coiled spring.

Read about Leonardo da Vinci (1452-1519). He drew a helicopter design many centuries before they were first built. His helicopter was spiral-shaped.

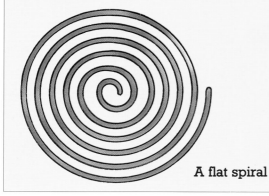

A flat spiral

A spring

Drawing a spiral

You will need: 8½×14 inch paper, ¼ inch graph paper, a ruler, a pencil, a protractor, a paper fastener, and a headed pin.

1. Draw two lines at right angles on a sheet of 8½×14 inch paper. Draw two more lines at 45° to the first lines.

Cut a strip of ¼ inch graph paper, 4×25 squares. Draw a line along the center of the strip. Mark a point on your line

3 squares from one end. Starting at the fifth square, number the points 1 to 20 along the line as shown.

2. Use a paper fastener to join your strip through the marked point to the point where your

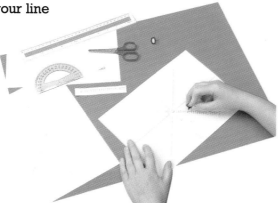

lines cross on the paper. This point will be the center of your spiral.

Use a pin to prick a hole at point 1 through the first line. Turn the strip to the next line and prick a hole through point 2. Turn the strip to the next line and prick a hole through point 3. Continue turning the strip one line at a time, pricking a hole at the next point. When you remove the strip you will have pricked out a spiral curve.

3. Join the holes with a pencil line. The spiral is growing by 1½ inches. Will it ever end?

A spiral flyer

You will need: ¼ inch graph paper, a compass, white paper, a pencil, felt-tip pens, glue, thin wooden sticks, and Fun Tak.

1. Draw a circle of radius 1¾ inches. Mark the center point. Draw 10 points at increasing distances (1, 1.5, 2, 2.5, 3, 3.5, 4 squares). Join the points to make a spiral.

Using this spiral as a guide, draw some spirals on white paper.

2. Pattern your spirals with felt-tip pens.

3. Cut out a decorated spiral. Cut along the curved line. Attach the center point to one end of a wooden stick and push the stick through a lower section so that your spiral is three dimensional. Secure with glue. Put a small piece of Fun Tak on the bottom end for a weight.

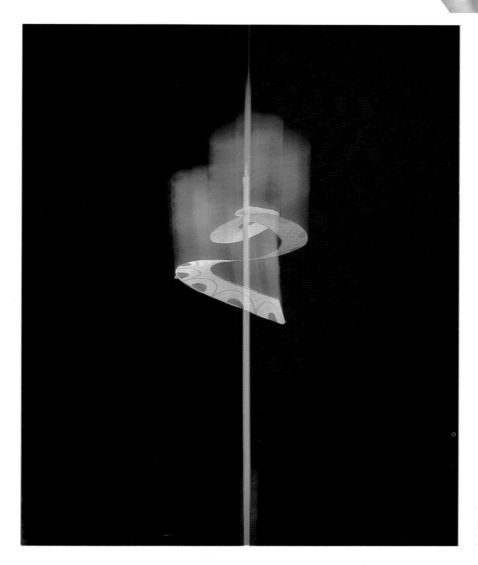

4. Stand on a chair and let your spiral flyer float down from a height. Notice the way it falls.

PENDULUM SWINGS

A pendulum is a suspended weight that swings freely around a fixed point.

Each swing takes a certain amount of time. The length of the pendulum determines the time of the swing. A long pendulum will swing more slowly than a shorter pendulum.

A pendulum travels in an arc of a circle as it moves.

Some clocks are operated by a pendulum.

Study a pendulum clock. Notice that the pendulum causes the tick-tock sound. Time keeping is adjusted by changing the length of the pendulum.

Find out about Galileo. He noticed that each swing of a suspended weight takes a fixed time. He suggested that this regular movement could be used to control a clock 70 years before the first pendulum clock was invented.

A swing pendulum

You will need: thin string and modeling clay.

1. Suspend a ball of modeling clay on a length of string. This is the pendulum's bob. Pull the bob a short distance toward yourself and let it go. Watch it swing.

2. Make a pendulum with string, length 16 inches. Set it swinging. Count the number of swings it makes in 10 seconds. Shorten your pendulum to 8 inches and repeat the experiment. Notice if this second pendulum swings faster or slower.

Record the number of swings in 10 seconds made by different length pendulums. Try a very short pendulum, and a very long one.

Make a colorful graph of your findings.

A rigid-arm pendulum

Some pendulums, such as those in a pendulum clock, have a rigid arm.

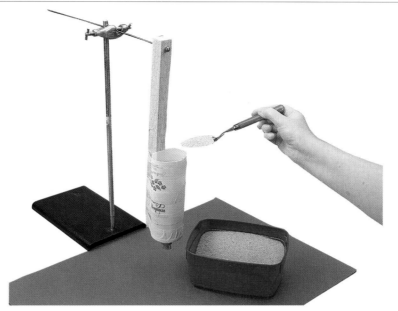

You will need: a length of balsa wood for a rod, a dishwashing liquid bottle, masking tape, scissors, a nail, sand, and paper.

1. Make a hole in one end of the balsa wood rod. Cut the bottom off the dishwashing liquid bottle and attach the bottle with masking tape to the other end of the rod. Put some sand in the bottle.

2. Working over a large sheet of paper, suspend your pendulum on a nail and pull the bottle towards you. Open the cap of the bottle and let the pendulum swing. The sand will sprinkle out and leave a trail. Notice the shape this trail leaves.

Swinging art

You will need: a dishwashing liquid bottle, scissors, thread, paints, and paper.

1. Cut the bottom off your dishwashing liquid bottle. This will be your paint dispenser. Make three holes near the edge and through these tie three equal lengths of thread. Suspend your pendulum as shown. Put some paint inside your dispenser.

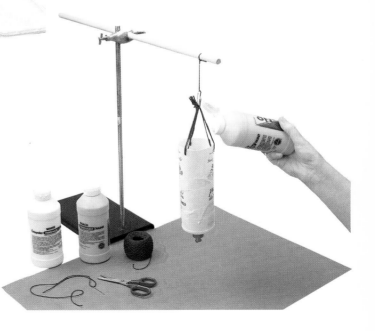

2. Work over a large sheet of paper. Open the cap of the bottle, and set your pendulum swinging.

The thread allows the pendulum to swing freely, and you will see loops, circles, and ellipses appear.

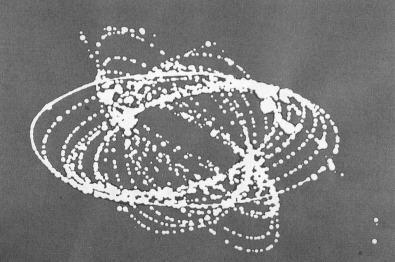

3. Swinging art.

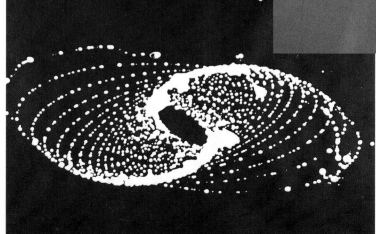

MOVEMENT AROUND AN AXIS

An axis is a straight line around which an object rotates. The earth turns around its north-south axis each day.

If a flat shape revolves around an axis it makes the shape of a three-dimensional symmetrical solid. The axis is the line of symmetry.

When you open a book, the spine is the axis. When you open a door, the hinge is the axis.

Look around a room. See how many things you can find that turn around an axis. See how many different hinges you can find.

Look in an atlas or study a globe. Try to find the world's north-south axis.

This semicircle shape creates the shape of a ball as it revolves around its axis.

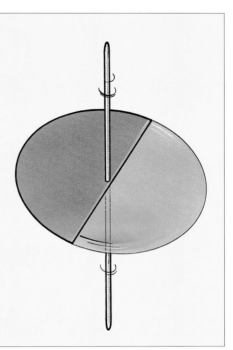

"The eggheads" – a hinged book

You will need: oak tag, cardboard, scissors, a pencil, a black pen (water resistant), colored inks or dyes.

1. Cut four sheets of oak tag, 5½×7¾ inches, for the pages of your book. Mark the center line on three of the pages – the fourth will be the cover of your book. Make a cardboard pattern of an egg shape. Use the pattern to draw an egg shape in the same position on each page.

2. With the black pen draw the eggs' heads above the line and their bodies below. Color your pictures with inks, paints, or dyes. If you allow the colors to blend together you will get interesting tones of color. Leave to dry, then cut two of the pages in half along the center line.

3. Make four holes on the left-hand side of the pages and tie them together to make a book. As you turn the pages they move in a circular movement around the axis.

4. Turn the half pages to make different eggheads! See how many egg people you can make?

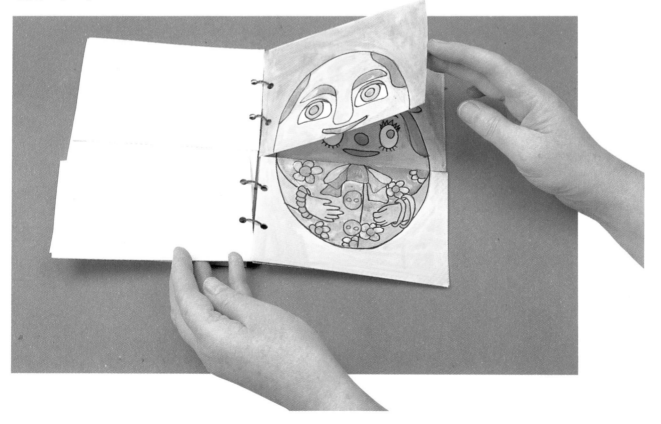

A hinged pop-up card

You will need: oak tag, scissors, a craft knife and safety ruler, felt-tip pens, a pencil, and glue.

1. Score and fold your oak tag in half. Draw your design on a smaller piece of oak tag.

2. Score and fold a strip of oak tag to form a box shape. The top rectangle must be exactly the same size as the base.

Glue the oak tag strip into the fold of your card as shown. Test to see if your card will fold flat, then leave to dry.

3. Cut out your design and glue it to the front of the folded box shape. As you open and close the card, the pop-up picture moves in a circular way around the card's folded hinges.

ROLLING

An object that moves forward by turning over and over is said to be rolling. Rolling objects move with a circular motion rotating around a center, like a ball, or around an axle, like a wheel.

An object that is smooth and round will roll easily downward if it is put on the top of a slope.

In art, paint rollers are used for decorating papers or for printing. The roller rotates around a central axle.

Try to do a forward roll on a soft surface such as grass or a gymnastics mat. Crouch down and sit on your heels. Then curl up, tuck your head well in, and roll forward and over.

If a car's brakes are released while it is standing on a slope, the car will roll forward.

Have you watched house decorators using a paint roller instead of a brush? A roller spreads paint more quickly and easily.

Which is easier – carrying this metal drum, or rolling it along the ground? Rolling it is easier.

Roller patterns

You will need: a print roller, printing inks and a tray, paper, leaves, and assorted textured materials.

1. Experiment with your roller and make some patterned papers.

2. Try lifting your roller up and down as you move along.

3. Roll across a leaf in one revolution. The leaf's pattern will imprint itself on the roller. As you continue to roll, a print is made of this impression which is a negative image of the leaf.

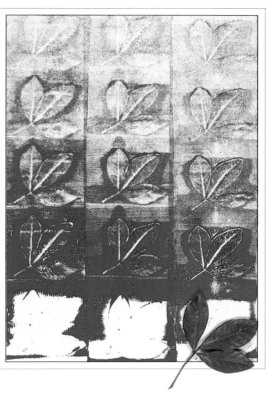

4. Try placing some leaves under the paper. These will show through as you roll over the surface of the paper. They will look dark with soft outlines. Try this with scraps of textured material, or papers such as plastic bubble wrap, burlap, or netting.

5. A roll-and-lift spiral.

A rolling test

1. Collect:
   - an assortment of objects
   - a cardboard cylinder and cone
   - a wagon body (see page 7)
   - a wagon with wheels

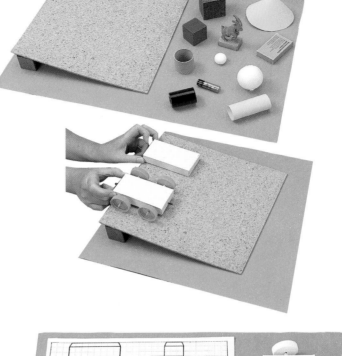

2. Make a ramp with a board and some blocks. Test each item to see if it rolls down the slope. See which rolls the easiest.

   Which of these wagons will roll down the slope?

An articulated wagon

You will need: oak tag, wooden sticks, a straw, 4 plastic bottle tops, glue, metal wire and pliers, and thread.

1. This wagon is the same size as the wagon on page 7, only it has been divided into two sections. It is made in the same way.

2. Join the two sections with a strip of oak tag, making a movable joint at one end with a small piece of wire. Attach the second joint. Do this before you glue the wagon bodies. Make a loop of thread at the front.

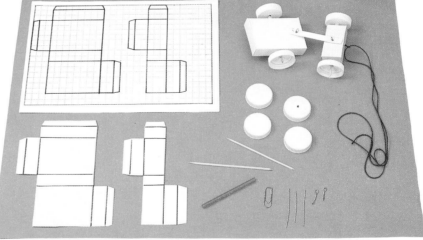

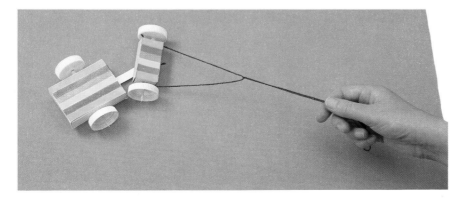

3. Because the wagon is jointed (articulated) it can change direction unlike the first wagon which could only travel in a straight line.

   Try turning your wagon to the left and right. See if it will turn in a circle.

Flexible materials will bend and stretch without breaking or tearing. Elastic materials are flexible. When they are stretched they will return to their original shape.

A spring is flexible. If a coiled metal spring is compressed – when its coils are squeezed together – the spring will bounce back into its normal shape.

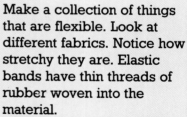

Early bicycles had no springs in their seats, and so were not very comfortable.

Make a collection of things that are flexible. Look at different fabrics. Notice how stretchy they are. Elastic bands have thin threads of rubber woven into the material.

Look closely at a bicycle seat. You will notice metal springs, making it more flexible. Think of other things that use metal springs.

Curl up small, then slowly uncurl and stretch up into the air. Your body is very flexible.

A paper spring

You will need: paper, scissors, a ruler, a pencil, and oak tag.

1. Cut several strips of paper (¾ inch wide). Place two strips at 90° to each other, and fold one across the other as shown. Continue to fold until all the paper is used.

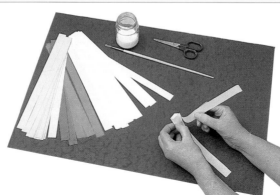

2. Put a spot of glue at each end so that the strips do not unwind.

Using two strips of different colors is fun. Watch how the twists move like a spiral as they unwind.

3. "A Jack-in-the-box card." Make a card with a tab that fits through the lower side. Stick your flexible strip to the center of the open card.

4. Make a face and glue it to the top square of the strip. Close the card.

5. Surprise your friends with your flexible Jack-in-the-box!

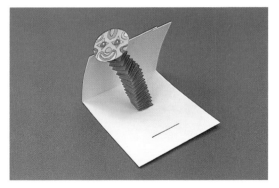

A metal spring

You will need: thin wire and a dowel rod.

1. Roll thin wire around a piece of dowel rod. You are making a spiral of wire. Remove the wire from the rod.

2. The coil of wire you have made will be flexible. It will bend and stretch. Stretch out your coil a little. Notice if it becomes more flexible.

A bendable man

You will need: your metal spring, a styrofoam ball, paints, colored adhesive-backed paper, yarn or fur, PVA glue, and modeling clay.

1. Paint the styrofoam ball and make a face with the colored adhesive-backed paper. Use PVA glue to stick on his hair of fur or yarn.

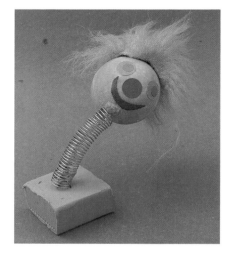

2. Push one end of your coil of wire into the head at the neck and the other end into a block of modeling clay. Watch him wobble.

An elastic scale

You will need: paper, ½ inch graph paper, scissors, a pencil, felt-tip pens, elastic, a yogurt cup, thread, a paper clip, wooden blocks or beads (or anything that can act as a weight).

1. Make a "number line" and attach it to a vertical stand or wall. Use a paper clip to attach the yogurt cup to one end of a piece of elastic. Make a loop of thread at the other end and suspend the elastic in front of your number line.

Note the level on the number line of the bottom of your elastic when it is unstretched.

2. Put a block or small **weight** into the cup and notice **how** much the elastic stretches. Continue to add weight and record the measurements.

3. Try your homemade scale using different elastic materials. You could use rubber bands. See if thick rubber bands stretch more than thin rubber bands.

A flexible table decoration

You will need: a plastic bottle, scissors, and modeling clay.

1. Cut the top off a plastic bottle. Cut down the side of the bottle so you have a lot of plastic strips.

Bend the strips outward and affix a little modeling clay at the tip of alternate strips. The plastic is flexible and will wave in the air if you move the bottle.

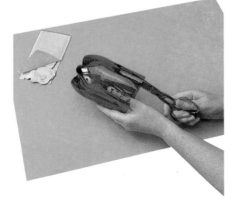

2. An unusual table decoration.

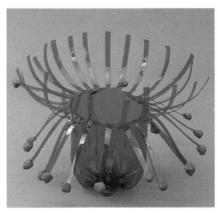

Sometimes the human eye appears to see something that is not really there. This is called an optical illusion.

Very fast movement can sometimes trick the eye into seeing images in unexpected ways.

Movies are really very fast sequences of still pictures. Each picture is slightly different from the picture before it, but they are moving so quickly that they give the illusion of continuous movement.

The next time you go to the movies, notice the projection room from which the reels of film are projected. Try to find out more about how a movie is made.

Try making your own moving picture book using a small notebook and a pencil.

Spinning disks

You will need: cardboard, a compass, a pencil, a ruler, a craft knife, felt-tip pens, scissors, wooden beads, a headed pin, and a balsa wood rod.

1. Draw two circles (radius 2¾ inches) on cardboard and with a compass and a pencil, divide your circles into six sectors. Draw a small circle (radius ½ inch) in the center. Using a half-moon-shaped pattern, draw a moon on each sector line. Draw them facing to the right on one circle, and to the left on the other.

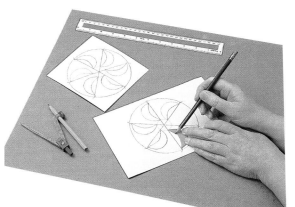

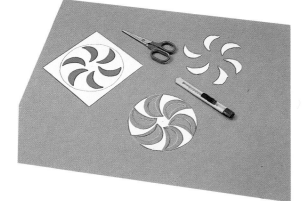

2. With a craft knife carefully cut out the moon segments of one circle. Color the outline of the moons. Cut out the circle. Color the moons on the second circle and leave this circle on a square background.

3. Use a headed pin to pin the square cardboard, and then the circular disk, onto the rod of balsa wood. Put beads between the disks to act as bearings. This will help them to spin more easily.

4. Spin the top disk and look through the moon holes. What do you see?

While the top disk is still spinning, spin the bottom square cardboard in the opposite direction. You will see interesting moving images.

Try to think of a new design of your own.

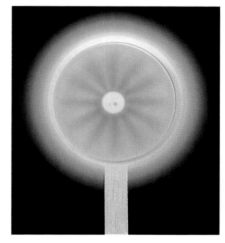

Moving spirals

Draw a spiral on another cardboard disk. Color it in contrasting colors. Spin it and watch the spiral move. Now spin it in the opposite direction. The spiral will seem to be growing, or moving in toward the center.

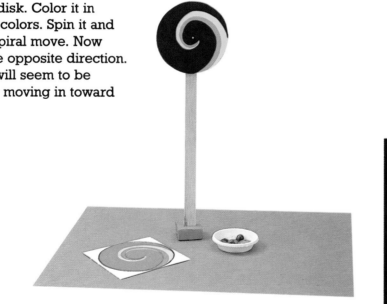

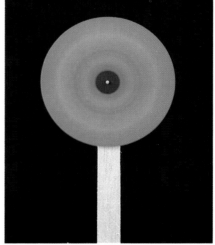

Watch the spiral as the disk slows down.

FURTHER IDEAS

An accordion snake

Cut out a snake in segments from oak tag. Color the snake and use paper fasteners for the joints of the body and the oak tag holding rods.

Make your snake bend and stretch and move up and down.

A rocking parrot

Make a parrot from cardboard. Use a round plate to draw the outline of the curved body. Paint it in bright colors. Punch a hole in the claw and suspend it on a knitting needle.

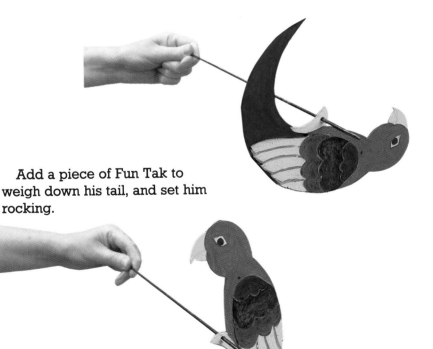

Add a piece of Fun Tak to weigh down his tail, and set him rocking.

An illustrated dictionary

Make an illustrated dictionary of words that have links with movement. Here are some examples:

skidding	roller skates
leaping	steam roller
bouncing	rolling stock
rolling	jelly roll

A photographic study

Use a camera to take photographs of things that move in our world. You could begin by using the ideas mentioned in each section of this book. With a video camera you could take moving pictures of your family and friends.

GLOSSARY

Articulated
Jointed. An articulated vehicle has jointed sections.

Axis
A straight line around which an object rotates

Circle
A round shape. All the points on the circumference of a circle are equidistant from the center point.

Elastic
Able to return to original size and shape after stretching

Ellipse
A closed curve. The sum of the distances of any point on the curve from the two focus points is the same.

Flexible
Able to change shape and bend without breaking

Force
A push or pull that can cause an object to move, stop, or change direction

Move
To change position

Movement
The process of moving: motion

Oscillate
To swing in a regular motion

Pendulum
A suspended weight that swings freely around a fixed point

Roll
To move by turning over and over

Rotate
To move around an axis or center

Spiral
To curve continuously around a fixed point at a steadily increasing distance

Spring
A device which, when compressed or bent, will return to its normal shape

Swing
To move back and forth or up and down

Vibrate
To move quickly back and forth or up and down

Additional photographs: Zefa 2-3, NHPA
(Stephen Dalton) 5.